Purgatory Has an Address

ROMAINE WASHINGTON

BAMBOO DART PRESS

LOS ANGELES † NEW YORK † LONDON † MELBOURNE

Purgatory Has an Address by Romaine Washington
ISBN: 978-1-947240-13-1
eISBN: 978-1-947240-14-8

Cover illustration and author photo by Marcus Muscato

For information:
Bamboo Dart Press
chapbooks@bamboodartpress.com
Curated and operated by Dennis Callaci and Mark Givens

Bamboo Dart Press 005

www.pelekinesis.com

www.bamboodartpress.com

www.shrimperrecords.com

Dedicated to Marcus and Mitchell

Contents

Long Afternoon

I am floating with balance wishing
 that one day
 we will walk in the park again.

~Mitchell Washington

What's Your Story?

mama said take those words
go on upstairs
see what you can make
the girl went up
came down
with a wadded ball of poetry
in her left eye
mama said get that out your eye
sent her back upstairs
the girl came down
with wadded balls
of poetry in both eyes
before mama could say anything
the girl opened her mouth
her tongue stretched
into a long rambling line of poetry
that filled up the room
poems swirled
around in the house
and spilled out the door

stopped at the feet
of an old man
with a shoppin' cart
in the street
talkin' about
how he met the goddess
of all things survived
and she was poem
and she was good
he turned his head
to stare at me
standin' underneath
a sycamore tree
and he asked . . .

Gargoyles and Goddesses

mom's perm potion
to magically take my hair
from afro crown to rapunzel flow
was a smoldering disaster

i shed from shoulder-length
to two tiny perpendicular pigtails
on either side of my toothless
seven-year-old smiling brown face.

to not feel so alone,
i cut the hair off all my dolls -
perfect plastics butchered
in a blond-don-king-heap-of-who-cares.

school laughter christened me ugly.
at recess i sat on the bench
with the girl taller
than anyone in our class
and the girl rounder
than anyone in our class.

we watched the desired-girls
giggling – running – whispering
looking our way.

looking at the boys –
i decided i wanted to play.
girls ran behind me,
boys ran around me,

as though i was a castle wall,
as though my head was a gargoyle
perched, ready to devour them
with my toothless roaring laugh.

i became a safe place
where girls with long hair
would scamper and squeal
as boys ran towards them.

i would growl like a gargoyle come to life.
boys ran away in fear
of being touched by someone unprettied.

i'd raise my arms, curl my fingers
as though i had claws. they'd run
when i gave my toothless dragon growl,
they'd run as though i had a gun.

i enlisted the help of my two new friends
and we became the protectors,
the safe place for all that is good
from all that is dangerous.

we belonged.
were a necessary force
like the gods and goddesses
we'd been studying.

invincible. we three,
christened ourselves
Artemis, Athena, and Hestia
– untouchable.

Disappearing Act - What's the Magic Word?

*avra kehdabra – i will create as I speak.
abbada ke dabra - perish like the word

1.
a woman enters a tall black box.
a gentleman in a tuxedo waves a wand.
taps the box twice. the woman disappears.
    she is hiding. we expect
    her reappearance
    under a brilliant spotlight.
she will end the night with a gracious curtsey,
magician holding her hand
as if she were a delicate trophy.

    he stands in moonlight,
    disillusioned head hung low,
    wand drooping in his fingers.

2.
a woman enters a tall black box of secrets,
avra kehdabra, the man flourishes a wand -
she disappears in an echo of laughter.

a baby appears on stage in her place.
the woman never returns.
this trick has no name.
the magician says,
i don't want to name it.
abbada ke dabra - he disappears.

3.
a magician emerges from a tall black box
a woman in a sparkling cheerleader outfit
waves a glittery silver wand above his head.
    she taps the black box
    twice on the side. we blink.
    she disappears. *ta-da*
a nameless toddler stands in her place,
with wand in hand,
trying to reach the lock on the tall black box.

4.
a man and a woman walk on stage together.
holding hands, they bow in unison.
no black box. no wand. they walk offstage.
    i dream i wake up and
    have a wand
a tall black empty box,
    avra kehdabra

I Go Back to the Middle of Your Kiss
After Sharon Olds

they are in their twenties
kissing outside a pool hall.
big d is daddy's
regiment nickname.
well-creased, smooth-edged,
6 foot one, with a son,
mississippi blues - mmhmm.

my mother is
new mexico brown,
5 foot 3,
loves to sway her hips
to any music that hits
her ears. that's how older
bro and sis were born.

she wraps her legs
'round his waist.
he blows a soft
something that sounds
like yes in her ear.

i want to stop them.
send her back home.
send him back
to the barracks.
i want to shout
you will be made
to do things
you will regret.
you will never see
each other again.

he won't be there
with sturdy shoulders
soldiering to protect you.
he will be awol - absent
without intent to desert.

you will have to give up
your third child.
you won't tell him
because you won't know
where he is.

you will be left alone.

i want to wedge myself

between your full lips
and say stop - but
i don't.

there is a father
from the west indies
and a mother
from ohio
waiting to adopt me
and
i need to be here.

"... Your Mother was a Good Catholic Girl"

adopted mom says it as though
her words will weave a magic connection
between me and you.

air smells of muted bronze and frankincense.
you are a brown silhouette kneeling in a pew,
rosary bead pinched between your fingers.

head bowed – eyes closed –
lips silently moving. wishing
time could swim backwards

Hail Mary
   Holy Mary
      Mother of God . . .

you did not want to be mother of me.
good catholic girls get lonely.
holy water does not wash loneliness away.

i am not the answer to your prayer.
but i want to be with you –
ease your loneliness.

a puddle of water
anoints your knees.
i am crowning.

you give me away.

Dream Breach

daddy's big hand
wraps around mama's cumulus ribs
his laughing bone
          spits into a tube of sun
daddy is a shadow
          of my unbelonging
his drunken shoes
shuffle down a one-way corridor
          where mama wails
          on the cusp of my being
i am an almost was
     hand sized / scraped out
          spineless fetus in amber mason jar
birthed from
an unkept promise
          i am a brown ripe baby
               swaddled in
                    sticky sheets
daddy floats away
          mama strains to hold him

her legs swallow dirt
        cracks the crook of her spine
the world is big and small at the same time
        i fall back on myself
no daddy hand   -   no mama hand
       to catch the fall

Nameless

my birth mom lives in san bernardino?
my birth mom lives in san francisco?
my birth mom lives in new mexico?
my birth mom lives in california?
my birth mom lives?
my birth mom?
my birth?
today
i ask for my
official birth
certificate
hoping for my
original birth
certificate

the one without secrets

the one that tells me
if she cared to name me
or was i baby girl - waiting
to be delivered - handed over

forgotten

the clerk tells me to wait
for my number to be called
right now i am a number

the clerk stands at the window
like the wizard of oz
pressing buttons

asks for a different name
where i was born
where my mother is from

as though i've had the answer
inside me all along
red shoes - chant - magic wand
air balloon to transport me
to the office of truth

the clerk decrees
your records are sealed
and they'll stay that way
you're gonna have to sit and wait

Fill in the Blanks

```
                        new mom? the first
          with your           question the
          new Name            registry asks
          know your              is your
          she doesn't            birth Name.
          you when               the second
          she gave               question
          the Name               asked is
          don't know             your birth
          when you               mother's
          her Name?              maiden
          don't know             Name.
          when you               question
          birth mom            marks.
          for your           on every
          you search        line un-
          how do          search-
                         able.
                         there
                         is a
                         potter's
                         field of
                         I don't
                         knows
                         buried
                         in a data
                         bank on
                         list serves
                         swirling
                         through

                      after birth
                      name?   how
                      no          do
                      with      you
                        search
```

Saguaro

A sneeze of wind
seeded me
purposeful accident
I take root
where the ground is
hard and angry
spits the sun
back in its face
drought drenched
tap root i
burrow beyond
ancestral bones
to anchor
a sturdy reservoir
of hope
where
i thrive
crowned

by brittle bites
of needles
and bloom

---

* SAGUARO A TYPE OF CACTUS THAT GROWS TALL/ LIVES 150-200
YEARS IS ABLE TO WITHSTAND DROUGHT AND HAS AN EFFICIENT ROOT
SYSTEM

My Name is a Banjo

i hear melon ripe names of African writers
and wonder what sounds would conjure my spirit
would i smile the same yes as when the world cooed
into the tiny river of question marks
of naming things as though they were
the sound of footprints in eyes

i am supposed to feel something
some connection
to remind me
that mama voice is god
and i am ashé

but i am no one's dream
named after no one no
roots - branches or leaves
avalanching into answers

when i swam in the soft belly
of sobbing pang
spanked on calf skin drum

plucked with
fat hot-fingered twang

my name is a banjo
a geechee cape
nana's sweaty nape
i belong to a place
i never knew

empty tin can
on a street corner
longing for the clink
of god's voice
ashé ashé
amen amen
awoman awoman
a baby girl
breached in
middle passage
where my ancestors'
names drowned
and god was.

Purgatory has an Address

mom said this place looks like
it tried to burn itself up
summers close enough to hell
to make her want to leave,
winters warm enough
to convince her to stay.

mom decides to make it lush,
'til dad's heart dies
in the middle of the sun,
mowing a neatly-planned
green-grass-dream
to please her.

buried. mom never
visits dad's lush lawn grave
for fear of not wanting
to leave. mom wants

to move but penance
is a slow process,
and there is nowhere
to go
where dreams
can promise
not to die.

Coloring Grid

tract homes planted next to a dairy farm
a neighborhood of neat mowed lawns
where all the faces are traced with red lines
colored with brown melanin.

the buyer's brochure did not reveal
the haze of cattle dung permeating
closed windows / shut doors,
incense fuming in each room.
fly strips dripping from porches like wind chimes.
feral cats gorging on wild mice.

yet gradually, the wreak of manure
becomes the familiar smell of home,
as sure as the itch and sneeze of cut grass,
the muffled sound of cattle grazing,
where methane clouds
drift through the value of our homes.

Where No Magnolias Bloom

there are no magnolias on magnolia street
an easy distraction from their absence
is the blanket of Kentucky bluegrass
cut by a barber with a straightedge razor

we swallow ice cool shadows of umbrella trees
shading the one-way tar-paved magnolia-less street
Madison-Franklin-Hancock streets are offshoots
bleeding from city planners' red-inked map

a southern twang sweat of boiling pig guts
fighting in the air with fermenting cow dung
from the farm next to our shiny tract homes
where no magnolias bloomed

on the corner bolted down was a big-blue-mailbox
where latchkey teens with shiny black smiles leaned
spitting whistles that stung my legs
wrapped themselves around my throat

at fourteen i learned the magic
of disappearing into sidewalk cracks
and the irony of street names
at the corner of no magnolias

Cul-de-sac is French

The bottom of a purse
    Possibly
    Loose change
    Possibility
    Of change
    Turn around
        Come out
From bottom
Framed in barbed wire
The crisscross top of steel
    Redlined

Uprooted
    Mom plants
    A laughing bush
    A pretty tease of poison
    Of pink and white
        Oleanders
A redlined ultimatum

Death is a bottomless black

But she believes in
    Balance
    Plants Italian Cypress
    In between Oleanders

Evergreen finger
    Pointing skyward
Taller than
    Pink and white blooms
    Barbed wire fences

Our eyes travel upward
    Recognizing hope
    When we scc it

Meditation in Dissolving Boundaries

The cow is a poem of compassion – Mahatma Gandhi

separated by barbed wire.
i sit on sleeping grass.
next door, you stand content in field.

air is drenched
with the soil-soaked stench
of baked dung.

horseflies hover around
your milkwhite-leatherbrown
shorthaired wall-of-body.

you fling your bovine tail
in languid swats
against your hips.

in summer heat
you bow down.
legs tucked beneath you.

large snout
pushes pouts
of heavy lazybreath.

leaf-sized umber ears
open wings pulling me into
your calm sepia gaze.

i am mesmerized by
the gentle way you chew
sun-soaked hay.

tasting and retasting,
you graze beyond barbed wire
swallowing the afternoon.

The Smoke of Patchouli

Nana Romaine and i relax
in a patchouli incense thread of smoke
floating through our strands of hair
braided with fingers and time
with nana there is always time
      a two-mile afternoon stroll
to barbara ann's sunshine colored bakery
coming home warm like oven
heavy with sleep
      nap wakes to front porch
evenings aproned
by the silk scent of yellow and pink rose bushes
in the cool-almost-dew
we snap green beans
      staccato pops in pots
   in the kitchen steam rises from giddy water
nana's house is cooking
late night pancakes
fried-chicken-and-mashed-potato mornings
sugar-dipped-dried-oranges & pickled-watermelon-rinds

nana and i eat what we want when we want
hours and days melt into obsession
as we unbox time in 1,000-piece jigsaw puzzles
memorizing edges / intricate rose gardens
blue & white & blue & white & blue & white sky pieces
that almost-fit-but-not-quite
a collage of thimbles
    dali's melting clocks
        dissolving into a stream
where memory stretches time
    weaves itself in and out of synapses
through decades
    as though nana was there when i was born
        pouring soft questions
            into my eyes

Decommissioned Norton AFB, 1994

remember the scorched air days
with me cocooned in the back seat of mama's car
staring up at your thin water tower legs
topped by an alien red and white checkered bubblehead
while she's in the commissary?
my high-heeled mom
puffin' on Virginia Slims
tippin' the boy who loads our car
brown paper bags that smell like pencil shavings
me wheezing and mom smoking at midnight
as she drives me to your hospital for asthma

i thought you were god exhaling
when your white wings cut clouds

everyone's stiffly creased uniforms and salutes
reminds me of my dad
black-clark-gable-lookin' major
with a chest full of pins and medals
who died before i could say his name

when you shut down
packed up and moved away
you were the closest thing to resurrection
i ever knew

All-American Pastime

sun is a blaring white ball of rays
beating us like a bat
 'til skin bleeds sweat

mouths full of heat
boys hack and spit
bus stop sidewalk

cop strolls over
book in hand
demands names

presses tickets to
14-year-old
    black boys' palms

penal code ———
ILLEGAL TO SPIT IN PUBLIC

we spit protest
sunflower seed chompin'

tobacco chewin' ballers   spit
boxers   rinse and spit
footballers   rinse and spit

cop blank stares us
ignorance
is no excuse

hand on belt
he turns his head - spits
a blaring white ball

foul on the way home
no umpire to intervene
we retreat to benches

learning the first strategy
in survival is knowing
who not to trust

the loud buzz
of a fat fly
threatens us to swat

the second strategy
in survival is knowing
when to swing

Incident in Blue

"Democracy must begin at home,
and its home is the neighborly community".

— Eric Klinenberg

maybe the dog pissed on the carpet one too many times
when the neighbor saw my son in the hot tub
and called the police

my son's head leaning back on his shoulders
eyes closed chest expanding in the water
the sun is god and he is god's well-baked son
eyes closed steeping like a soaked chamomile tea bag
ready for dreams

eyes open
two police stiffly stand over him
        get out of the jacuzzi, sir
he is yanked into a nightmare

the sun shifts to shadows on the pavement
my bare-chest barefoot wallet-less son
stepped out calmly

makes sure not to give the allusion of a weapon
do nothing to make them nervous

We had a complaint from the complex
about a vagrant in the jacuzzi

... and the sun is yellow dog-piss raining on him
voice clear - but not too firm
    I live here - I can take you to my condo
My son's hazel eyes scan neighbors' windows
police are relaxed – and satisfied

on the phone
i hear rage shaking in his voice
    i'm no punk - in no mood- to see you
    i look like mr. clean- but I'm no punk...
his mind paces
    a neighbor called – the police –
    i gotta calm down... ...
i can feel his tears punching holes in walls
    i'm no punk... had to stay calm...
    the police— i gotta calm down
    but not today

Bre'r Boombox

I

Leroy an' 'em got clean wild laughs
like air full of jokes an' afro picks.
i never hear they mama tell 'em be safe -
come home, but know she do.
they a little older than me.
don't really know 'em - but feel like i do,
like the bus be a two-hundred-year-old boat
we been ridin' too long.
i lean my head full of tired sun
against the window.

bus stop. door belches open.
Leroy an' 'em loud talkin' thud walkin'
claim territory in the back of the bus,
boom box blastin', *wave your hands in the air* -
feel like there's no air in here,
but Leroy laugh like cool grass an' green trees.

> *hey driver, why we*
> *ain't got no air in here?*

black Mack, our reg'lar driver woulda made a joke.
like he, be part of we - be fam.
Leroy would lean back, put headphones on,
bop - quiet smile satisfied.

II
Hank is white shirt, small frame,
lookin' like sweat don't know his name.
type o' man who might chuckle
but never heave a full laugh,
if he did you might think he was passin' gas.
wasn't one of us in talk-skin-deed or thought,
never had to strategize to get what he want.
    he rearviewin' Leroy without a clue
    of what to say or do:
        You need to hold that noise down.
        You're disturbing the other passengers.
Leroy laughs a little too loud and long.
            Hank's face is beet

but he don't call for back up.
          does not back up.
      stands his ground.
      he parks.
white pants walk stern
to the back of de bus.

orders Leroy an' 'em:
>   *kill the sound. or get off.*

Leroy an' 'em look like they murder just for fun.

>   *who you think you talkin' to l'il man?*
>   *i paid like e'erbody else.*
>   *go on up an' drive.*
no one say nothin'.
i face forward.
quick scuffle.

Leroy an' 'em jump off de bus
afro picks bobbin' in the air
boombox clutched to chest
bass beatin' fear in feet.
they fly into invisible.
i wanna say
>   *Leroy this ain't what it means to be a man,*

but that moment be gone.

i stare at flies hoverin' o'er stabbed
beads of blood.

Disappearing Act II

a performer walks on stage
    opens her mouth as if to sing
black question marks explode from her teeth.

the audience pulls out umbrellas.
    the performer can't see their faces.
she closes her mouth and walks off stage.

*

a performer walks on stage,
    pulls out an umbrella,
recites verses from the Quran.

the audience chants *we can't hear you*
    hurls crosses at her.
she picks up a cross and walks off stage.

*

a performer walks on stage
    a tattooed cross on her back.
arms horizontal, head bowed, feet crossed.

the audience explodes in raucous laughter.
    teeth tumble out their mouths
shattering at her feet - she walks off stage.

a performer walks on stage
    gathers shards of teeth
throws them up like confetti

the audience weeps. walks away.
    she stands center stage.
alone.

From Inside a Burning Building

i am writing from inside a burning building.
the cell phone in the corner keeps asking,
how am i doing? what do i see?
does it hurt as bad as it smells?

i have lost my sense of smell,
but understand
we must document these things
because we are here and still alive.

my hair is charcoal.
skin is peeling layers of tears.
scientists say the skin weeps
when it is badly burned.

the air tastes like tires
though i have never tasted a tire,
this is how i imagine it tastes.

this is what i must tell the cell phone
so, it has a simile to understand,

there are really no words to describe
how it feels to be inside a burning building.

there are no words to capture,
the sensation of walls eating you alive.

i look at windows exploding
knowing they will be there tomorrow,
the same time,
ready to explode again.

my cell phone rings,
Covid is calling from a hospital bed.

i cannot visit my friend
whose fever is so high
she is hallucinating.

she says:
i am sweat
pouring from my eyes,
yelling at me,
"there are stories to be written."

she says,
i am sorry,
but i can't.

she hangs up the phone.
tomorrow she is telling me
it feels good to be quarantined
where the sheets are white,
and the quiet is eating me alive.

Burning Bush

we are stubborn tumbleweeds
Arroyo's withered innocence
etched in sun a burning need

orange groves long deceased
business howls a ghosted din
we are stubborn tumbleweeds

rooted in what used to be
dreams of safe suburban bliss
etched in sun a burning need

despite hope's drought we will not leave
hollow malls and blaring wind
we are stubborn tumbleweeds

thorny eyes scrape lonely streets
where homeless hide in shivered pitch
etched in sun a vicious need

murder floods Arroyo's creek
while school kids sit in restless desks
we are stubborn tumbleweeds
etched in sun a burning need

at the end of the devil's breath

July.
Wilted cereal in a bowl / we
Drown in brown milk.
The haze of sparklers and fire-
Works add to the deafening heat
That drips into

August.
Caged in by smog,
Air smells of cigarettes
and black exhaust.
Surely this place
is meant to Ignite.

September.
When he arrives,
He thinks this is a flat plain,
Where desert dirt covers
everything like snow
And sweat is meant for
breathing.
But then –

October.
And the devil's breath laps up lotion,
Claws skin with its vicious teeth.
Yowling roofs beat whoosh and
Bend of threatened windows.
Tree leaves sound like ocean.
Stripped-dry, littered bare limbs.
The hard ones, snap - ripe for a switch.
Usedtabe gangs of tumbleweeds
ran the streets;
Now solitary wadded balls
of rootless limbs roll by.

November.
Is a postcard miracle,
Surrounded snow cap crisp sky
Where our eyes hang glide like eagles.
We perch low in the valley shadow
Straining to see the walk of fame,
Sunset and Hollywood,
Palm Springs.
Peer into the pier of the Pacific.
Every mountain peak is
Paramount. He says

If it weren't for the devil's breath,
I'd never know where we are, and
Just how beautiful.

ACKNOWLEDGMENTS

The following poems in this collection previously appeared, in one form or another, in the following publications:

Gargoyles and Goddesses, From Inside a Burning Building - *Pandemic Summer Chapbook*. I Go to the Middle of Your Kiss, Purgatory has an Address, The Smoke of Patchouli - *Cholla Needles 39*. Cul-de-Sac is French - *San Bernardino Singing*. All-American Pastime, Br'er Boombox, Saguaro - *Cholla Needles 36*. Meditations in Dissolving Boundaries, Coloring Grid - *Cholla Needles 32*. Burning Bush - *Redlands Review*. at the end of the devil's breath - *San Bernardino Singing, Accolades*, and *Voicemail Poems*

About the Author

Romaine Washington, M. Ed. is the author of *Sirens in Her Belly* (2015, Jamii Publications). She is a fellow of The Watering Hole, South Carolina and the Inland Area Writing Project at the University of California Riverside. She is an active member of the poetry community in the Inland Empire. Washington is an educator and a native Californian from San Bernardino.

AUTHOR PHOTO BY MARCUS MUSCATO

112 N. Harvard Ave. #65
Claremont, CA 91711
chapbooks@bamboodartpress.com
www.bamboodartpress.com

CPSIA information can be obtained
at www.ICGtesting.com
Printed in the USA
BVHW070112280622
640646BV00004B/47

9 781947 240131